NIGERIA
the culture

Anne Rosenberg

A Bobbie Kalman Book

The Lands, Peoples, and Cultures Series

 Crabtree Publishing Company

www.crabtreebooks.com

The Lands, Peoples, and Cultures Series

Created by Bobbie Kalman

Coordinating editor
Ellen Rodger

Project development, photoresearch, and design
First Folio Resource Group, Inc.
Erinn Banting
Pauline Beggs
Tom Dart
Kathryn Lane
Claire Milne
Debbie Smith

Editing
Jessica Rudolph

Separations and film
Embassy Graphics

Printer
Worzalla Publishing Company

Consultants
Ibrahim Hamza, York University; Olatunji Ojo, York University

Photographs
Brian Brahe/Photo Researchers: cover; Corbis/Paul Almasy: p. 8 (both), p. 25 (top), p. 26 (left), p. 27 (both); Corbis/The Bowers Museum of Cultural Art: p. 26 (right); Corbis/Contemporary African Art Collection: p. 20 (bottom); Corbis/Jerry Cooke: p. 14 (top); Corbis/Werner Forman: p. 7 (bottom); Robert Frerck/Odyssey Productions: p. 18 (bottom); Juliet Highet/The Hutchison Library: p. 3, p. 7 (top left), p. 17 (right), p. 22, p. 23 (top left); George Holton/Photo Researchers: p. 7 (top right), p. 14 (bottom);

The Hutchison Library: title page, p. 10 (both), p. 11 (bottom), p. 12, p. 13 (both), p. 15 (right), p. 19 (top), p. 21 (top), p. 24 (top), p. 25 (bottom); Jason Lauré: p. 17 (left), p. 23 (bottom), p. 24 (bottom); Giles Moberly/Impact: p. 5 (top); James Morris/Panos Pictures: p. 5 (bottom), p. 9 (bottom), p. 11 (top), p. 18 (top), p. 20 (top), p. 23 (top right), p. 28; John Moss/Photo Researchers: p. 19 (bottom); Bruce Paton/Panos Pictures: p. 6; Giacomo Pirozzi/Panos Pictures: p. 4 (top), p. 16 (top); Betty Press/Panos Pictures: p. 16 (bottom), p. 21 (bottom); J. Reditt/The Hutchison Library: p. 15 (left); Reuters/Brian Snyder/Archive Photos: p. 29 (both); Marcus Rose/Panos Pictures: p. 4 (bottom); Candace Scharsu: p. 9 (top)

Illustrations
Dianne Eastman: icon
Kristi Frost: pp. 30-31
David Wysotski, Allure Illustrations: back cover

Cover: A group of musicians play traditional instruments at a festival in Katsina.

Title page: People dance and play drums at a celebration in Jos.

Icon: A terracotta mask appears at the head of each section.

Back cover: Bush babies live in Nigeria's rainforests and savannas.

Published by
Crabtree Publishing Company

PMB 16A
350 Fifth Avenue
Suite 3308
New York
N.Y. 10118

612 Welland Avenue
St. Catharines
Ontario, Canada
L2M 5V6

73 Lime Walk
Headington
Oxford OX3 7AD
United Kingdom

Cataloging in Publication Data
Rosenberg, Anne, 1964–
Nigeria, the culture / Anne Rosenberg.
p. cm. -- (The lands, peoples, and cultures series)
Includes index.
ISBN 0-86505-249-2 (rlb.) -- ISBN 0-86505-329-4 (pbk.)
1. Nigeria--Civilization--Juvenile literature. [1. Nigeria--Social life and customs.]I.
Title. II. Series.

DT515.4 .R67 2000
966.9--dc21

00-043226
LC

Contents

Children gather in Kaduna, in northern Nigeria.

More people live in Nigeria than in any other country on the African continent. Their **ancestors** settled on the land thousands of years ago. Some came to trade their goods; others were looking for a new home where food and water were plentiful. Today, Nigeria's people belong to over 470 **ethnic groups**, each with its own background and culture. The largest ethnic groups are the Fulani, Hausa, Igbo, and Yoruba peoples.

A woman grinds red pigment, or dye, which she will use to decorate clay pots.

Old and new

The religious beliefs, celebrations, art, music, and literature of Nigeria's people are a mix of the old and the new. Some people believe in many gods like their ancient ancestors did, while others follow religions that came to Nigeria more recently. Traditional masked dancers celebrate the harvest, while young people in western-style clothes dance in the cities' nightclubs. The haunting rhythms of *kalangu* drums and rattles echo alongside the lively sounds of rock music and *juju*. This blend of traditions adds to the richness of Nigeria's culture.

(right) A man carries water on his head in a giant clay pot.

(below) People play drums, sing, and dance in front of a brightly painted wall at a community center in Abuja.

Religion plays an important part in the lives of most Nigerians. Fifty percent of the population are Muslim and forty percent are Christian, but hundreds of traditional African religions are also observed. Often, Muslims or Christians combine their faiths with traditional beliefs.

Traditional beliefs

Nigerians' earliest religious beliefs were based on animism. Animists believe that objects in nature have souls. Some souls or spirits are powerful, such as the spirits of rivers or lightning. Other spirits, such as those of trees, are weak.

Natural objects are considered **sacred**, or holy. Before using these objects, animists must seek the spirits' permission. For example, if animists want to fish in a river, they must first make **offerings**, gifts of food or flowers, to the spirit of the river.

Huge wooden carvings decorate the
entrance to a shrine in Oshogbo.

Gods and goddesses

Nigeria's many animist religions believe in a supreme god who created the earth. The Yoruba call their highest god Olorun, meaning "owner of the sky." Traditional religions also **worship** other gods and goddesses, who are believed to reward those who honor them and punish those who disobey them. Nigerians build shrines, places dedicated to a god, where they pray, bring offerings, and seek the god's advice.

The Sacred Forest

Many African religions treat the forest as the house of the gods. The famous Sacred Forest, near the southwestern town of Oshogbo, is filled with shrines to Yoruba gods and goddesses. One of the most impressive shrines is that of Oshun, goddess of the Oshun River. Oshun is also the goddess of **fertility**. Women pray to her in the belief that she will give them many children. The god Ifa, who some believe can predict the future, is also honored in the Sacred Forest. Each day, visitors ask him for advice about their lives.

A statue of the goddess Oshun stands beside the Oshun River in the Sacred Forest.

Ancestor worship

Ancestor worship plays an important role in traditional Nigerian religions. Followers believe that the souls of their ancestors remain on earth and influence their families' daily lives. If the ancestors are happy, they will bring successful harvests and healthy children. If the ancestors are angry, they may cause ill health or poor crops. To worship their ancestors, people pray or make offerings at **altars**.

This ancient Igbo stone carving represents a family's ancestor.

Totems

Members of traditional religions believe that their families are descended from the spirits of objects found in nature. The animal or plant that is a family's ancestor is called a totem. People often carry small carvings of their totems, which identify them as members of a particular family or group. A family's totem is considered sacred. For example, if a family's totem is a lion, family members are forbidden to harm lions.

A totem in the shape of a lion was worn as a bracelet during the thirteenth century, in the ancient kingdom of Benin.

Islam

Between the seventh and fifteenth centuries, traders from Arabia spread Islam throughout North and West Africa. Today, almost half of all Nigerians are Muslims, followers of Islam. The largest Muslim groups are the Hausa and Fulani peoples of northern Nigeria and the Kanuri people of Borno, in northeastern Nigeria.

Islam was founded by the **prophet** Muhammad, who received and spread the teachings of Allah, the Arabic name for God. Allah's teachings are recorded in the Qur'an, the Muslim holy book. The religion has five main principles, known as the Five Pillars of Islam. Muslims must declare that Allah is the only god and that Muhammad is his prophet. They must pray five times a day facing the holy city of Mecca, in Saudi Arabia, where Muhammad was born. They are required to **fast** during daylight hours in the holy month of Ramadan and to give part of their income to the poor. The final pillar is to perform the *Hajj*, a **pilgrimage** to Mecca.

A young girl reads part of the Qur'an, written on a tablet, to her friends.

A group of Muslim men pray on mats in a small mosque in Ibadan.

Christianity

In the fifteenth century, European missionaries, people who are sent to other countries to spread religion, brought Christianity to Nigeria. Like Muslims, Christians believe in one god. Their religion is based on the teachings of Jesus Christ, who is believed to be God's son on earth. His lessons are recorded in the Christian holy book called the New Testament.

Today, the Igbo, along with many other Nigerian peoples, are Christians. Some people have started their own churches, called Aladura churches, which blend Christian ideas with traditional religious beliefs. In Aladura churches, for example, people say prayers from the New Testament, but they also pray to the spirits of their ancestors to help them in times of illness.

(right) A woman dances toward an offering box which is used to hold money that Christians donate to their church.

(below) Hundreds of Christians attend a church service in Benin City, in southern Nigeria.

Amulets

Nigerians of all faiths wear amulets, or charms, on bracelets or necklaces. They believe that these powerful and holy objects cure disease and keep away evil spirits. Amulets are usually made of leather or metal. Some are carved in the shape of wild animals, while others are decorated with interesting designs. Muslims' amulets are called *layu* and have a verse from the Qur'an inside.

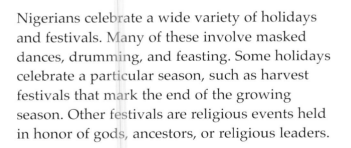

A year of celebrations

Nigerians celebrate a wide variety of holidays and festivals. Many of these involve masked dances, drumming, and feasting. Some holidays celebrate a particular season, such as harvest festivals that mark the end of the growing season. Other festivals are religious events held in honor of gods, ancestors, or religious leaders.

A new season

In September, when the new season's yams are ready, the Igbo hold a harvest festival called Ikeji. During the festival, they give thanks to the yam spirit, Ihejioku, for a successful harvest. Many towns gather for the festival. Each one presents a dance or a piece of music, and a panel of judges chooses the best performance.

(right) A man with a painted face performs at a festival honoring the Yoruba god of iron.

(below) People gather in the town of Warri, in southern Nigeria, to celebrate the new year.

Women dressed in colorful costumes play instruments and dance at a celebration in Benin City.

A fishing festival

The Argungu Fishing Festival takes place on the banks of the Sokoto River, near the town of Argungu in northwest Nigeria. Thousands of people take part in a fishing contest to mark the beginning of the fishing season. When the event begins, they race toward the river carrying fishing nets and large **gourds**. Then, they dive into the river in a fierce competition for the largest fish. The fish is given to the *emir* of Argungu, the king and Muslim religious leader who organizes the festival. To make sure there are enough fish for this event, part of the river is closed off to fishing during the year. Though the most important part of the festival is the fishing contest, duck hunting, diving competitions, and canoe races are also popular events.

Hundreds of fishermen with gourds and nets try to catch the biggest fish in the Sokoto River.

Muslims pray outside their mosque, or house of worship, during Ramadan. So many people have come to pray that there is no room left inside.

Oshun

The Yoruba hold festivals for each of their gods. One of their most sacred festivals honors Oshun. Every August, thousands of people gather at the banks of the Oshun River to worship the goddess of fertility. Women collect water from the sacred river and pray to Oshun for many children.

Igue

The festival of Igue is celebrated by the Edo people every December in Benin City, in southern Nigeria. Igue honors the *oba*, the king of Benin City. During this seven-day festival, people fight make-believe battles and perform traditional dances to show loyalty to their leader. On the last day of Igue, children gather leaves from the forest, called "leaves of joy," to bring happiness to their families.

Ramadan

Ramadan is the ninth month of the Muslim calendar. It is considered the holiest month of the year because it was then that Allah first revealed the words of the Qur'an to Muhammad. During Ramadan, adults and older children fast from sunrise to sunset. Muslims believe that fasting teaches **self-discipline** and helps them appreciate Allah's blessings. At night, the fast is broken with a festive meal. With the end of Ramadan comes the beginning of Eid al-Fitr, the Festival of Fast-Breaking, which is celebrated with parades and feasts.

Cycles of the moon

The Muslim year is based on the lunar calendar, which follows the cycles of the moon. When a new moon appears, a new month begins. The lunar year has only 355 days, 10 days less than the solar calendar used in North America, so a Muslim holiday that falls in spring one year may fall in winter years later.

A colorful parade

A major part of most Muslim festivals is the *durbar*. The *durbar* is a tribute to the *emirs*. It begins with a parade, which hundreds of thousands of people flock to see. Men dressed in coats of armor and copper helmets ride on horses decorated with rich gold and silver cloth. Riding in the center of the parade is the *emir,* who is dressed in flowing white robes and is shielded from the hot sun with an umbrella or parasol. Ornately dressed drummers and **lute** players follow the colorful procession. The day ends with a huge feast while musicians entertain the crowds.

Christmas and Easter

Christmas and Easter are the two most important Christian holidays. Christmas celebrates the day that Jesus Christ was born. On December 25, people go to church to pray, and then gather with family and friends for feasting and dancing. Easter, held in April, marks Jesus' death and **resurrection**. The holiday begins on Good Friday, the day Jesus died. It is a quiet and solemn day when Christians attend church services. Easter Sunday, the day on which Christians believe Jesus rose from the dead, is a joyous occasion, celebrated with feasting, dancing, and **masquerades**.

(left) During a **durbar,** *the* **Emir of Katsina,** *in northern Nigeria, parades through the streets beneath a bright red and yellow umbrella.*

(below) People sing, play instruments, and parade through the streets on Sallah Day, a Muslim festival.

Nigerians enjoy celebrating special occasions, such as births and weddings, with their friends and family. These celebrations differ from one culture to another, but music, dancing, and feasting always play an important part.

A Yoruba naming ceremony

For the Yoruba, like other Nigerian people, naming a baby is an important event. They believe that a baby must be named within seven to nine days after it is born. Otherwise, a baby boy will not live longer than his father and a baby girl will not live longer than her mother. Friends gather at the family's house for the baby naming ceremony. The baby's foot is touched to the ground, to symbolize its first steps in the right direction. Guests bring food and gifts for the baby, and prayers are recited for the child's health. The parents then choose the baby's name. This name sometimes expresses wishes for the child's future. For example, the name Arike means "one who is blessed."

Getting married

On the day of a traditional Nigerian wedding ceremony, the bride and groom dress in their finest clothes. They exchange rings and repeat the words "they will ripen" to symbolize their growth as a couple. The two then share a **kola** nut as a symbol of their union, and sugar and honey is passed around to the guests to make sure that the marriage will be sweet. When the ceremony is over, the bride and groom kneel with their families to say prayers, and guests enjoy a huge wedding feast.

An Ondo girl has painted her face for a coming of age ceremony, which marks her passage into womanhood.

A man and woman marry at the city hall in Abuja, in central Nigeria.

The bride price

In traditional cultures, the groom's family is expected to give the bride's family a gift to make up for the loss of their daughter. A part of this, or sometimes the whole amount, is then given to the couple, who use it to set up their new home. Although paid in money today, this gift, called a bride price, was once paid in cattle or cowrie shells. Cowrie shells are seashells that were used in place of money.

Ogoji

For Nigerians, growing older is a sign of greatness. Fortieth birthdays are particularly special. Family and friends are invited to a big party called an *ogoji*. People even fly in from other parts of the world to attend. Guests shower the 40-year-old with money and gifts to show their affection and support. Afterwards, they enjoy a huge feast of lamb or goat meat, and dance until the early hours of the morning.

Polygamy

Both Islam and traditional African religions allow a man to have more than one wife at the same time. Some Nigerian men marry up to four wives. The practice of marrying more than one wife, called polygamy, developed so that men could have many children. You can often tell if a man has more than one wife by the clothes that the women wear. Wives of the same husband will wear dresses made of the same material, though the styles of the dresses may be different.

Beautifully carved sculptures mark peoples' graves.

Celebrating loved ones

Many Nigerians believe that death is not an end, but a journey into the **afterlife**. When someone dies, family and friends gather to remember and celebrate that person's life. The body is carefully bathed because it must be clean before the soul can join its ancestors. A woman's hair is braided, and a man's hair is shaved or combed neatly. On the day of the burial, relatives form a procession to the grave. Dressed in beautiful clothes, the person who died is placed in the grave along with food, drink, beads, or money. It is believed that the dead will need these objects in their next life.

The clothing people wear every day reflects their ways of life. Nigerians who live in cities often wear western-style clothing such as jeans or T-shirts. Many people in the countryside wear the traditional costumes of their ethnic group. Traditional outfits in Nigeria are usually long, loose, and flowing. This helps protect people from the sun and keeps them cool in hot weather.

Everyday clothes

One of the most common articles of clothing for women is a wrap-around skirt. To wear these skirts, women fold a long piece of cloth, wrap it around their hips or waist, and tie it in a knot, letting the long lengths of leftover fabric hang to one side. Women often wear the skirts with long-sleeved blouses and heavy sashes, which they use to carry packages. Mothers sling these sashes across their backs and go about their business with their babies tucked cozily inside. Men wear long-sleeved shirts and loose, comfortable pants. On their feet, most people wear sandals, though in rural areas people often go barefoot.

(top) Girls at a village near Kano wear brightly colored skirts, dresses, shirts, and headscarves.

Lots of hats

A common sight throughout the countryside are huge, broad-rimmed hats that extend over the shoulders to provide shade. Other hats, such as the ones worn by the Fulani, have rounded tops with wavy brims. Yoruba women wear a *gele*, a piece of brightly patterned cloth that is wrapped around the head. Some say that the way a woman wears her *gele* tells others what mood she is in.

A man wears an intricately woven hat.

So many beads!

In Nigeria, both men and women wear beaded necklaces, earrings, bracelets, and anklets. Beads are not only for decoration. They also give information about the person wearing them. For example, some beaded costumes indicate whether a girl is married or not. Beads are also worn during important events such as births, weddings, and funerals.

(right) A girl wears a metal hoop, shells, and strands of beads in her hair.

*(below) Many **obas** wear elaborate headdresses made from thousands of beads.*

Hairstyles

Many Nigerian women have elaborate hairstyles. Some weave heavy brass ornaments into their hair or wear many rows of tiny braids in fancy patterns. These hairstyles are thought to bring out a woman's beauty and make her look younger. Some hairstyles tell whether or not a woman is married. For example, in the north, many unmarried women wear their hair in a bun, while married women dangle a pigtail over their foreheads.

Clothing and Islam

Very religious Muslims must act and dress modestly so that they do not draw attention to themselves. In Nigeria, religious Muslim women wear long, dark robes and scarves to cover their hair. Men dress in layers of long silk or cotton robes. On special occasions, these may include a *riga,* a wide, pleated gown decorated with beautiful embroidery. The number of layers a man wears indicates how wealthy he is.

Arts and crafts

Nigerians have created exquisite art for thousands of years. In the ancient kingdoms of Benin and Ile-Ife, for example, artists made bronze statues and brass figures that became famous around the world. Today, artists still practice ancient arts as well as traditional crafts such as weaving and woodcarving.

Casting

Nigerians have a long tradition of shaping liquid bronze and brass into sculptures. This process is known as casting. Artists first create a sculpture out of wax, then put clay around it to make a mold. The mold is heated to melt the wax, which flows out of a hole in the bottom. Melted bronze is then poured into the empty mold. When the metal cools, artists break the mold to reveal the bronze sculpture inside.

(above) A terracotta carving shows an ancient warrior from the kingdom of Benin.

(left) Melted brass is carefully poured into a wax mold.

Sculpting

Nigerians use bronze, iron, wood, and even mud to make sculptures. Some ethnic groups believe that they can communicate with the gods through these sculptures, and village chiefs display them as symbols of their power. Professional artists create most sculptures, but in many areas, sculpting is a family activity that young children learn from their parents.

A secret art

The Igbo have practiced the ancient art of blacksmithing, or shaping objects from iron, since prehistoric times. Today, Igbo ironworkers make hoes, knives, and other tools, keeping their techniques closely guarded secrets. Their finest pieces of work are iron rattles. These rattles are sculpted into animal figures such as birds, cows, or snakes, and are used in Igbo funeral ceremonies.

A sculptor carves delicate designs into the bottom of a clay pot.

Kasali Akambi, a Yoruba sculptor, carves a giant mask at his workshop in Kano.

Weaving

Nigerians use a variety of materials in their weaving. Fulani weavers make warm blankets, or *khasa*, out of sheep's wool and camel hair. Nigerians across the country weave colorful yarns into blankets or sleeping mats, and straw and grasses into baskets. Not all weaving is done by hand. Cotton, wool, rayon, and silk are woven into cloth using weaving machines called looms.

This painting, called "Masked People Around a Cauldron," was created by Emmanuel Ekong Ekefrey. This self-taught artist uses Nigerian myths and symbols in his work.

A man weaves beautiful blue cloth on a loom.

Colorful cloths

For centuries, Nigerians have used dye to create colorful patterns on cloth. One of the oldest and most common dyes used in Nigeria is called indigo. This deep blue dye comes from the indigo plant. The northern city of Kano and the southern city of Abeokuta are famous for their dye pits, which are deep holes in the ground filled with dye.

(left) To get just the right color, people dip their cloth into Kano's dye pits many times, letting the cloth dry between each dip.

(below) An artist uses a wax stick to draw patterns on cloth. When she dyes the cloth, only the parts on which she drew will stay white. This technique is called batik.

Making music

In Nigeria, music plays an important part in everyday life. Farmers, fishermen, and **laborers** each have their own work songs. Nigerians also sing for fun and to bring good luck. They use songs in their prayers and celebrations. Each special occasion has a distinct type of music. There are songs for births, weddings, funerals, and even songs to welcome visitors.

A mix of styles

Each ethnic group has a different style of traditional music, although many instruments are common to all groups. The instruments are usually made of local materials such as shells, animal skins, and wood.

At the beginning of the twentieth century, European and American sailors brought the music of their countries to Nigeria's ports. Local musicians blended traditional African rattles and drums with acoustic guitars, creating the country's earliest form of western-style popular music.

Drums

Nigeria's most important musical instrument is the drum. Most ceremonies involve drums, and their beat echoes in the country's nightclubs. Drums come in many shapes and sizes. They are usually made from wood, with goatskin or cowhide stretched over the top.

One of the most popular drums is the hourglass-shaped *kalangu* drum. To play it, musicians wedge the drum under their arms and strike it with their fingers or a small stick. By pressing the cords that connect the drum's top and bottom, players can change its **pitch**. The *kalangu* is often called "the talking drum" because experienced players can make it imitate the rise and fall of the human voice.

King Sunny Ade

Sunny Ade plays a lively style of music known as *juju. Juju* combines the traditional *kalangu* drum with guitar and voice. Through music, Ade shares his hope that the problems between ethnic groups in Nigeria will end. In 1977, entertainment journalists, recording companies, and thousands of his fans began calling Ade "The King of *Juju.*" Since he received this honor, people simply call him "King Sunny."

A boy holds a **tama** *drum before a performance in Abuja.*

*The Gbaggi Kabulo Ensemble plays traditional Nigerian instruments such as **goras.***

Femi Kuti sings at a concert in New York City.

The Kuti family

Fela Kuti, one of Nigeria's most respected musicians, created Afrobeat, a popular form of Nigerian music that combines traditional African styles with American soul music. Fela sang about government **corruption** and injustice. His opposition to Nigeria's military governments led to his arrest in 1985. After his arrest, Fela's son, Femi, also a musician, took over his father's band. Today, Femi leads his own band, called "Positive Force." Like his father, who died in 1997, he uses his songs to speak out against political corruption and to encourage black youth to be proud of their African ancestry.

A woman shakes a hollow gourd covered by beads to make a sound like a rattle.

Gora

Many Nigerian musicians play the *gora,* also called a *sekere.* This instrument is made from a gourd and has a long wooden neck with 21 strings. Players hold the *gora* in their lap and pluck its strings with their thumbs and index fingers. Using their knuckles, musicians can also make rapping sounds on the body of the *gora.* This is a difficult instrument to learn, so *gora* players often begin lessons at a very young age.

Thumb piano

The thumb piano, called a *sanza* or *bolo,* is another popular instrument. Thumb pianos are made of short strips of metal fastened to a wooden box. They can even be made by fastening umbrella spokes to pieces of wood! To play the *sanza,* musicians hold the box in both hands and pluck the strips with their thumbs. Each metal strip is a different length. The shorter the strip, the higher the sound.

Care to dance?

Nigerian dances often tell stories or describe historical events. Some are a way to mark a special occasion or to communicate with the gods or one's ancestors. Dance is also a form of entertainment. People love to dance until the early hours of the morning in Nigeria's many nightclubs.

(above) Traditional dancers and singers perform at a festival in Kano.

(top) Yoruba girls dance at a festival in Katsina.

Ceremonial dances

Dance is an important part of many Nigerian ceremonies. The Igbo hold ceremonies in which dancers walk through water to appeal to the water spirits for good luck. Dance also adds to the grand spectacle of the *durbar*. Hausa and Fulani dancers leap and spin past the crowds to clear a path for the *emir*, who follows on horseback.

Ceremonial dances also mark important events in people's lives. They welcome a child into the world, ensure a successful hunt, or celebrate a young man's coming into manhood. Young Fulani men hoping to attract a mate perform the *yaake* dance. Wearing colorful eye makeup and elaborate costumes, they roll their eyes and dance on tiptoe for many hours. At Yoruba burial ceremonies, men dance on the grave, making great stomping movements to pack the earth into place.

Agricultural dances

Some dances mark the end of the growing season by giving thanks to the gods for a successful crop. The Irigwe people of the north perform one dance in which they leap high in the air to represent the growth of the crops. When crops fail, dances act as prayers in which people ask the gods for better harvests in the coming seasons.

Work dances

Laborers perform dances to help them through long hours of work or to celebrate the end of projects. In Nigeria, there are dances for every type of work. For example, Nigerian fishermen create dances using the broad, sweeping movements of throwing a net. The dances of Igbo blacksmiths mimic the steady swing of the hammer as it strikes the iron. Hunters dance by copying the movements of the animals they hunt.

(right) Two women dance the night away at an outdoor party.

(below) The River State Dancers, a traditional dance troupe in Nigeria, perform in Lagos.

Dancing the highlife

During the 1920s, a new type of music, called highlife, became popular. It combined guitars with rattles, drums, and other traditional instruments. When people heard this music, they created a dance to go with it. Partners would "mirror" one another, or imitate each other's movements as they swayed their hips and shoulders to the rhythm of the music.

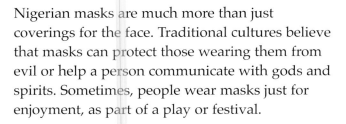
Nigerian masks are much more than just coverings for the face. Traditional cultures believe that masks can protect those wearing them from evil or help a person communicate with gods and spirits. Sometimes, people wear masks just for enjoyment, as part of a play or festival.

Making masks

Nigerian masks are made from all sorts of materials, including wood, brass, leather, cloth, ivory, and beads. Maskmakers follow rules that are handed down from generation to generation. One rule says that if maskmakers want to carve a wooden mask, they must first bless the tree so as not to offend the spirits. Another rule says that maskmakers must be careful when handling masks. If they are not gentle, the masks will frown to show their displeasure.

A girl wearing a painted clay mask dances while her friends play drums, a rattle, and a tambourine.

An ancient Igbo mask has a face made of metal and a headpiece made of brightly painted wood.

A variety of masks

Masks are worn in various ways. Some masks cover only the face. Others cover the wearer from head to toe. Still others are even taller than the people wearing them! Many masks are worn around the hips or waist. These masks are usually part of an elaborate costume made of cloth, plant fibers, or beads.

What is that?

Masks represent different things. They might have carved features that look like a person or they could be shaped like an animal, symbolizing the powerful spirits of nature. Artists often combine the features of people and animals, believing that this will allow them to control the spirits of wild animals.

A dancer at a masquerade in Kano wears a covering made of woven grasses over his entire body.

Masquerades

Masquerades are ceremonies in which dancers wear masks and costumes. Some masquerades act out a request to the gods, for example, a request for a good harvest. Masquerades are also performed to honor people or animals. The Fulani perform masquerades to honor their cattle, whose movements they imitate as part of the dance. Masquerades also provide guidance. At Yoruba burial masquerades, dancers in flowing robes and elaborately carved headpieces lead the spirits of the dead toward their ancestors.

A performer wearing a colorful headdress shakes a rattle while he dances.

Language and literature

More than 400 languages are spoken in Nigeria. English is the country's official language. The other main languages are Hausa in the north, Igbo in the southeast, and Yoruba in the southwest. Many Nigerians speak three or four languages. For example, the pastoral Fulani, who travel through the country for part of the year looking for food and water for their cattle, speak mainly Fulfulde, but they also speak the languages of the people on whose land their cattle feed.

A bookstore in Kaduna uses English for its signs.

Yoruba

Yoruba, spoken by the Yoruba people, is a tonal language. Changes in the pitch of a speaker's voice change the meaning of a word. For example, the word *oro* may mean fruit, celebration, or punishment, depending on whether the speaker uses a high, medium, or low pitch.

Igbo

There are over 200 Igbo groups in Nigeria and they speak more than 30 dialects, or variations of their language. As a result, Igbo people from different regions cannot always understand one another.

Hausa

Hausa is spoken mainly by the Hausa people and other groups in northern Nigeria, as well as by some peoples in the southwest. Hausa can be written using two different alphabets. In books and newspapers, Hausa is written using the Roman alphabet, which is the one used for English. When writing poetry, it is common for the Hausa to use the Arabic alphabet.

English	Hausa	Yoruba	Igbo
Hello	*Sannu*	*Bawo ni*	*Igbola*
Goodbye	*Sai wataranu*	*O dabo*	*Ka omesia*
Good morning	*Barka da kwana*	*E ku aaro*	*Ibolachi*
How are you?	*Lafiya?*	*Bawo ni?*	*Keedu?*
I am fine	*Lafiya lau*	*Daadaa ni*	*Ee, adi m mma*
Please	*Don allah*	*Jowo*	*Biko*
Thank you	*Yauwa*	*E se e*	*Imena*
You're welcome	*Baa koomi*	*E wo le*	*I mezie la*
Yes	*Toh*	*Bee ni*	*eee*
No	*A a*	*Bee ko*	*mba*

Which language?

Not only do Nigerians often speak several languages, but sometimes they switch from one language to another in the middle of a conversation! This practice, called code switching, usually happens when the subject changes. Some speakers even change languages in the middle of a sentence!

Wole Soyinka

Nigeria's authors describe life in their country in short stories, plays, novels, and poems. Born in 1934, Wole Soyinka, a member of the Yoruba people, is one of Nigeria's most famous authors. His many novels and plays are written in English. One of his best-known works, *A Dance of the Forests,* celebrates Nigeria's independence from Britain. Soyinka has also been an outspoken critic of Nigeria's military governments. As a result, the Nigerian government banned several of his books. In 1967, he was arrested and imprisoned for two years. In 1986, Soyinka became the first African writer to win the Nobel Prize for literature.

Wole Soyinka listens to a speech at a ceremony being held in his honor.

Chinua Achebe has published many books of stories and poems, including a book for children called **How the Leopard Got His Claws.**

Chinua Achebe

Chinua Achebe, a member of the Igbo people, was born in 1930. Like Wole Soyinka, he writes his novels, short stories, and plays in English. One of his most important works is his first novel, *Things Fall Apart.* When Achebe wrote *Things Fall Apart,* he was concerned that people around the world had mistaken ideas about Nigeria. Most had only learned about the country by reading books written by non-Africans. These books often had incorrect information in them. Achebe hoped that *Things Fall Apart* would correct their false impressions. *Things Fall Apart* sold millions of copies worldwide and is now taught in schools throughout the world.

Nigerians love to tell stories about their history. Most of their stories are not written, but are passed orally from one generation to another. Many of these tales are myths and legends that describe how the earth was created. Here is one version of a Yoruba creation myth.

In the beginning

In the beginning, there was no solid land. There was only sky above and vast stretches of water below.

Olorun, the Supreme Creator, ruled over the sky and all that lay beneath. One day, he looked at the grayness below. "Ah," he sighed, "this place is nothing but water and air. How dreary it all is. I will go and ask Obatala, my son, to create land and fill the world with human beings."

"Obatala," he said. "The world is an empty place. Go and create land and shape human beings."

"A wonderful idea," Obatala agreed. "But how?"

"Here are the things you will need," Olorun answered, handing his son a long silver chain, a bag full of sand, and a chicken. Obatala attached one end of the chain to the heavens and lowered the other end to the world below. Ever so slowly, he climbed down the chain. There was no place to step when he reached the bottom, so Obatala poured the sand over the sea. Reaching into his bag, he pulled out the chicken and placed it carefully on the sand. The chicken scratched at it, spreading sand in all directions and forming valleys and mountains.

The earth still had no people, so Obatala dug some clay out of the ground and began to mold men and women. He worked for many days and nights. Creating people was tiring, so he sat down to rest. Just then, Olorun appeared to see how things were coming along. "Olorun," said Obatala, "I have molded man and woman, but they are nothing but clay figures. They do not breathe."

"I will blow life into them," Olorun answered. Taking a deep breath, he filled his lungs and blew on the clay figures. Obatala and Olorun watched with joy as the color rose in the people's cheeks. One by one, the people stood up, dusted themselves off, and prepared to begin their work. "We have no tools," they said to one another. So, Olorun gave them hoes to plant their crops and bows and arrows to hunt for food.

The people cheered and set about their business. They planted their crops and hunted for antelope and wild deer. Olorun saw that his work was done. He climbed the silver chain to heaven, tucking it into his pocket after him so people could not follow. As for Obatala, Olorun rewarded him by making his son the first king of Ile-Ife, where the world was created.

Glossary

afterlife Life after death

altar A table or stand used for religious ceremonies

ancestor A person from whom one is descended

corruption Dishonesty, especially bribery

emir A Muslim king or religious leader

ethnic group A group of people who share a common race, language, heritage, or religion

fast To stop eating food or certain kinds of food for religious or health reasons

fertility The ability to produce children

gourd The hard-shelled fruit of certain vines, which is dried and used to make cups, bowls, and other utensils

kola A tropical tree found in West Africa that produces nuts used to make soft drinks

laborer A person whose work requires strength

lute A stringed musical instrument

masquerade A ceremony at which everyone wears a costume and a mask

oba A king

offering A gift presented to a god as a sign of worship

pilgrimage A journey made for religious reasons

pitch The highness or lowness of a sound

prophet A person who is believed to speak on behalf of a god

resurrection Rising from the dead or coming back to life

sacred Having special religious importance

self-discipline The ability to control one's feelings and actions

worship To honor or respect a god

Index

1 2 3 4 5 6 7 8 9 0   Printed in the USA   5 4 3 2 1 0 9 8 7 6

9/06,4

9/06,4